HEALTH HEROES

I'M A CUSTODIAN

LAUREN KUKLA

ILLUSTRATED BY **NADIA GUNAWAN**

MAYO CLINIC PRESS KIDS

With gratitude to Liah Olsen, Environmental Services Technician

MAYO CLINIC PRESS KIDS | An imprint of Mayo Clinic Press
200 First St. SW
Rochester, MN 55905
MCPress.MayoClinic.org

To stay informed about Mayo Clinic Press, please subscribe to our free e-newsletter at MCPress.MayoClinic.org or follow us on social media.

For bulk sales contact Mayo Clinic at SpecialSalesMayoBooks@mayo.edu.

Proceeds from the sale of every book benefit important medical research and education at Mayo Clinic.

ISBN: 9798887701028 (paperback) | 9798887701011 (library binding) | 9798887701523 (ebook) | 9798887701233 (multiuser PDF) | 9798887701035 (multiuser ePub)

Library of Congress Control Number: 2023023813
Library of Congress Cataloging-in-Publication Data is available upon request.

TABLE OF CONTENTS

CHAPTER 1

HELLO!

Hello! My name is Gabe Tan. I'm a hospital custodian! I help keep the hospital clean.

I love my job because I create a safe environment for people who aren't feeling well. I also get to see lots of different people. Every day, I try to make at least three people smile.

Custodians work in museums, airports, schools, and more. Some work in healthcare settings like hospitals and **clinics**. I work for a large hospital.

HOSPITAL

I clean the hospital's public spaces, restrooms, and patient rooms. Many of the patients at the hospital are very sick. Being exposed to **viruses** and **bacteria** could make them even sicker. My job helps keep patients safe.

CHAPTER 2

A CUSTODIAN'S TOOL KIT

Being a custodian takes special skills. Custodians need to pay close attention to details. Custodians that work in healthcare need to have compassion for patients. But there are also tools that help me do my job. I store these tools in a handy cart. When I'm working, it goes wherever I go!

DISINFECTING WIPES

To **sanitize** surfaces

MOP

EXTRA GLOVES AND MASKS

PAPER TOWELS AND TOILET PAPER

To restock restrooms

BROOM

CLEANING SOLUTIONS
To clean different surfaces and spills

TABLET
For hospital staff to tell me which areas need cleaning

TRASH BAG

9

I work with other members of my healthcare team to keep the hospital clean. **Meet some of the people on the team!**

MARA

NURSE

Tells me when a patient room needs to be cleaned

ALEX
HOSPITAL GREETER
Tells me about messes in entrances or restrooms

ABDUL
SECURITY
Tells me about messes in waiting areas and hallways

11

CHAPTER 3

A DAY AS A CUSTODIAN

My day starts bright and early in the morning.

6:45 AM

I park my car in the ramp and head into the hospital. I change into my work uniform. I put on my badge.

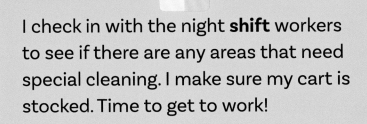

7:00 AM

I check in with the night **shift** workers to see if there are any areas that need special cleaning. I make sure my cart is stocked. Time to get to work!

7:15 AM

I start by cleaning the main entrance. I sweep the floor and mop it. I put up a sign to mark the wet floor. I don't want anyone to slip!

CAUTION

WET FLOOR

14

8:30 AM

I clean one of the restrooms. I wait until it is empty. I use **disinfecting** wipes on the counters and sinks. I clean the toilets. I restock paper towels and toilet paper. I check to make sure I didn't miss anything.

9:45 AM

Abdul tells me a little boy spilled a drink in the **ER** waiting room. I head over to clean it up.

"Don't worry!" I tell the boy. "I'll have this cleaned up in no time."

The boy smiles.

I stop by the hospital's welcome desk to talk to Alex. They tell me about some restrooms that need a little extra attention today. I refill the face masks and hand sanitizer at Alex's desk.

10:30 AM

17

11:35 AM

It starts raining outside. That means wet, muddy feet! I clean the entrance again to make sure no one slips.

"Let me get the door for you," I say to a family coming in.

12:30 PM

After a lunch break, I take the elevator up to the **pediatric** floor. Mara says they need help with checkouts. That means cleaning rooms after patients have been **discharged**.

"Can you push six for me?" I ask a little girl in the elevator.

The girl smiles and pushes the elevator button.

19

1:00 PM

I prepare a room for the next patient. I take out the trash. I change the bedding. I make sure the floor, counters, and bathroom are spotless. I even wipe down the TV remote. The room is ready!

2:30 PM

I clean some rooms with patients in them. I knock on a door.

"Is it okay if I come in to tidy your room?" I ask.

The boy inside says yes.

When I'm done, I thank him for letting me clean. "Do you need anything before I go?" I ask.

3:30 PM

Emily often stays at the hospital during her cancer treatments. She loves watching soccer. So do I! We talk about the latest game while I clean her room.

4:15 PM

I clean the hospital's entrances and restrooms one more time. I restock my cart before getting ready to head home.

CHAPTER 4

PATIENTS COME FIRST

Before leaving for the day, I check in with the night shift custodian. Nadia just started her job. She is still learning.

I stay late to help Nadia clean a waiting room. I want to make sure she is comfortable before she works on her own. Nadia smiles and thanks me for my help.

Being a hospital custodian isn't always easy. The job can be messy. It can be hard to see patients who are hurt or sick.

Still, I love my job. My work helps keep people healthy and safe. Every day, I go home knowing I've made a difference.

REAL-LIFE HERO!

MEET A REAL-LIFE CUSTODIAN!

NAME: Liah Olsen

JOB: Environmental Services Technician/Housekeeping

PLACE OF WORK: Mayo Clinic

What is your favorite part of being a hospital custodian?

I love just about everything about my job! I get to interact with lots of different people every day. Doctors and nurses often tell me how much they appreciate me helping keep their patients safe. This makes me feel good. I also enjoy the feeling of satisfaction I get when I finish cleaning a room. I know that I've done a good job, and the next patient to come in here will be pleased.

What does a hospital custodian do?

My personal mission is to create a safe environment for those who are not feeling well. When patients come here, I want them to know they will be safe. I keep them safe by cleaning high-touch and high-traffic areas. I also keep patients comfortable by making sure their rooms are tidy and well stocked.

What is the hardest part about being a hospital custodian?

The most challenging part of my job is what I call "sandy season." This happens in wintertime, when people are constantly bringing in snow, sand, mud, and other gunk from the roads and sidewalks. It is never-ending!

What character traits do you think it's important for hospital custodians to have?

Hospital custodians must show respect and compassion to everyone they meet. I know that hospital patients are **vulnerable**. I want to make sure they feel safe when they are here. I want them to know they can trust me.

COMPASSION

Health heroes have special superpowers that help them do their jobs. One of a hospital custodian's most important superpowers is compassion! I understand that patients don't feel well and may be scared or upset. I help them any way I can. I ask if they need anything. I find them a nurse when they need one. By treating patients with compassion, I help make their hospital stays as comfortable as possible.

HOW DO YOU SHOW COMPASSION?

GLOSSARY

bacteria—tiny living things made up of just one cell. Some types of bacteria can cause disease.

clinic—a healthcare building where patients have scheduled visits with healthcare providers

discharge—to release from something, such as a hospital's care

disinfect—to clean with chemicals that destroy germs

ER—emergency room. The ER is the department of a hospital that treats patients who need to receive care right away.

pediatric—relating to healthcare for young people

sanitize—to remove as many germs as possible from surfaces

shift—a scheduled period of time that a person is at work

virus—a type of germ that multiplies in living cells, such as the cells of the human body, and causes disease

vulnerable—easily hurt or affected by something and needing special care or protection

LEARN MORE

KSTP. "Unsung Heroes of COVID-19: Hospital Housekeepers." https://kstp.com/kstp -news/top-news/unsung-heroes-of-covid-19-hospital-housekeepers/

Manley, Erika S. *Custodians*. Minneapolis: Jump!, 2018.

Mayo Clinic In the Loop. "More Than a Clean Room: Custodian Connects Patient to a Piece of Her Past." https://intheloop.mayoclinic.org/2022/03/24/more-than-a -clean-room-custodian-connects-patient-to-a-piece-of-her-past/

Murray, Julie. *Custodians*. Minneapolis: Abdo Kids, 2021.

Rossiter, Brienna. *We Need Health Care Workers*. Lake Elmo, MN: Focus Readers, 2022.

INDEX